thawing

by Katherine Bryant

Published by: Post Oak Publications
P.O. Box 70455
Nashville, TN 37207-0455
(615) 227-4562
(615) 228-8073 (Fax)

Library of Congress Catalog Card Number: 98-67019

International Standard Book Number: 0-9620115-9-2

Photo Credits: Thawing (cover) by Sydonie Bryant Kopels
Gathering Winter Berries by McCurdy Lipsey
Watching Eagles and Wood Nymphs by John Bowers
Springing Forth by Sydonie Bryant Kopels
Feeling for Natural Elements by John Bowers
Author Photo by McCurdy Lipsey
Thawing (back cover) by Sydonie Bryant Kopels

Text Design: Maria Smith, Smith-Lenoir Graphic Creations

First Printing: December 1999

dedication

To John Bowers, for always

i'd like to thank

First, I must say that Emma Wisdom is not only a fine editor and publisher but a friend willing to swap roles whenever necessary. My mother, Ruth Bryant, is always the first reader and even if I sometimes ignore her changes, I consider her the best judge. Next, the members of my writers' group—Jim, Frank, Dana, and sometimes David and Mack, have always given their candid and later their seasoned responses. And finally, honors to my daughter Sydonie, the girl with a wonderful eye, and my son Zachary, the boy with an emerging spirit. Thanks to you all.

preface

All my life I've written poetry in journals, scattered poems on the backs of cocktail napkins and paper bags, losing them in the messes of my daily life. Although I've made my living writing and teaching prose, it is my poetry that has been under wraps since the earlier part of my life *when the language of my heart was open*. That language closed when I was sixteen and I became interested in journalism. My well meaning English teacher spurred me on to be a journalist, discouraging my poetic tendencies because they "didn't pay." I shut them away for twenty-eight years.

Then in the winter of my forty-fourth year, *I cracked open*. The only sounds I heard in the silence of my pain and my eventual recovery were those of my heart—its poetry.

The title of this book, **Thawing**, mirrors the meltdown I had to experience before I could again hear or share my words with others. In the first section, **Gathering Winter Berries**, I pick up the pieces of my former life as a woman, and a lover of language and nature. I begin a search that has since changed my life—forever. I look at the history and metaphors of my existence and try to make sense of them; try to be freed from and by them. I end a long term relationship and offer myself up to the Goddess of Maybe. I search for physical and emotional strength as I take stock of the valuable parts of myself.

In **Watching Eagles and Nymphs**, I find my form. I search the woods and skies for creatures like me. On one prophetic walk near a lake near home, I discover a twenty-year friendship is more than just a friendship. At that very moment, the ice-crusts of the lake begin to break as the warmer air hits the watery surfaces. A sound—like tiny windchimes—charms both me and my friend but we remain silent with each other. Then he hears me say something which I don't speak aloud—and the most important relationship of my life emerges.

Springing Forth details the surges of love for nature and the man I've found. They recreate me. I become passionate again—in love, involved in the natural world—I find places I'd never dreamed existed. I am washed clean with my own blood and feeling. *Transcendence occurs*.

Finally, **Feeling for Natural Elements** reaches into the future and pulls me back into the balance of work and love, art and philosophy. I hear the tunes from past places. I travel into my roots. I mourn the loss of loved ones and lost ones. I try to set the place for me in the world. *Harmony results*.

The writing of poetry, this book in particular, maps my journey for two years. Snapshots of my personal changes are superimposed over the larger landscapes of which I am part in the fabric of all existence. I have learned to speak again; learned to love again; learned to wait and create. I do not believe in explaining poetry—*it just is*. But perhaps these brackets can help a passing reader understand the framework I used. The message and the meaning, however, come from the language of the poetry.

Katherine Bryant, Nashville, TN
July 1998

table of contents

gathering winter berries

watching eagles and nymphs

springing forth

feeling for natural elements

gathering winter berries

being alone after important men

I am trying to learn to be in love with myself -
to know the patterns of my own quiet voices,
to feel the rhythms of my own fleshed psyche,
to self-contain, self-attend, self-create

(constantly)

Riding waves of days that wash away mistakes
in tears and forgiveness,
tides rising from inside my child
and the parent who nurtures it.

(I)

Blend joy and pain to a fine powder
of daily existence and time-to-time

(knowing)

It is the constant mortar of my being

(meanwhile)

I wait for no man,
Watch for no one,
but myself.

a hole

There's a hole in the fabric of my life,
a tear at the breast, a run in the leg.

My skin longs to be free of its garment,
wanting to be whole again, scrubbed clean.

But things are missing, open rips bleed,
I feel them stretched and numbed.

These skeined dye lots will not match,
the weave of wool hangs in wet patches.

At times I long to be used, worn again,
in a rich pink tapestry rewoven.

My warp is hopelessly flawed, gaping,
unwoven in silent splendor.

my shell

Flesh-pink nautilus, rolling itself against the battling sea,
My water tides toughen in their rocking need to be.

I gather chain-mailed strength to war, fight standing solo,
I long for shores of rest, to stretch my guts over warm sand.

No one, nothing comes into me beyond the smooth porcelain,
except another starfished creature who plays inside me.

Subtle and quiet, he opens to my seasonal tides as they crack,
entering the core of my softness from all sides, making pools.

I wait for the next wave, alone against vast weathers crashing,
remembering secrets in motion, visits from flesh and storm.

Today begins another tempest in my hard won life, unopened,
the future forms of memory, security, and the changing sea.

sisters weaving, brothers speaking at the memorial for lost children

Crowds, clouds gather
to celebrate a family of children
slain, silent, returned to earth.

A tiny garden planted
with many-colored blooms
ranunculus, daisy, primula.

We wait for spring
listening to thunder and guns
named by victims' families left in tones.

Elysia Kathleen Coghlan, 16
Adriane Nicole Dickerson, 12
Jerimayer Divine Warfield, 12

Homicide, infanticide remembered
by many raced and gendered peoples-
sisters weaving, brothers speaking.

The family of man and woman
knows no colors except the flowers
sees no pain except the sky's showers.

God cries for slain babies,
ministers don't explain but swing
incense and prayer into the air.

The audience sways,
remembering children suffered,
injustices of other humans.

We bond to the garden,
under tents and umbrellas,
in the joy borne from healing.

The children rise again
on petals of rain and tears,
cheeks and hands joined.

We all say:
We dedicate this Children's Memorial Garden in the spirit of love and compassion,
in the hope that someone passing by may find relief from their journey.
Amen.

my children, again

In the golden part of my eye, I can see my babies again
Waddling and paddling in summer waters
Round brown bodies and tiny barley teeth.
Water babies open in my golden locket, forever trapped
In happiness and languid love
Sealed in amber like aquatic insects caught in time and space.

Hours and hours of watching them, waiting
For growth and learning, in plastic pools
Swimming pools with tots in polka dot suits
Creamy yogurt and orange juice popsicles.
Changes from play school into middle school rampages
Shocked me, too much growth crashing over my smooth-rocked privacies.

Apart, I see her now with my face, laughing at me
Under makeup eyes behind which lives that baby laughing.
In him I see those chubby-creased arms reaching
For me rather than hard armed sinews under black t-shirts.
Summer again, my babies go away, to their own splashing streams
And I am left alone, opening the locket of our past
Hoping that someday they'll see me again with golden eyes.

my son is

My son is... a turtle hiding in the mud
emerging from the bottom of the earth
with pond-brown tattoos on his shell and toes.

He comes to snap, loll, stretch on sunny sticks,
he's sure in swimming, slow in waking -
subtle in open landscapes, careful of marauders.

His talents rise in after-hibernation doings,
his opportunities multiply in close marsh waters -
and he grows stronger as springlife approaches.

He practices paced strokes, watching others,
his strength of knowing, certainty growing,
he opens the monocle of the lake in his soul.

My son is a turtle moving out of the mud into the sun.
Go.

grandmother's tables

I converse-
of materialism in reverse.
I wonder now
whether things own me, perverse.

He asks why-
I need this stuff of life around me.
I think of dispossessing, planning
to move it, get myself free.

Then wood speaks-
I polish hard, listening to repasts.
I hear them, singing hymns
smell the lemon wax of my past.

I see grandmothers-
ghosts in matching wingchairs.
I hear their softcloths
on the maple-table, reflecting my redhair.

It is artforms-
passed down hand-to-hand.
From old women, dead but living
in new ones rubbing to understand.

I know them-
all the shes of my childhood,
circling with me over antique carvings
in cherry, oak, chestnut, and rosewood.

transitions in bed

White pillows in downed stacks on the antique bed,
the bed we were all conceived in years ago.

Folds of Amish quilts, black with azure under amber,
strands to beauty and function in the world.

I drink darkroasted coffees and eat sweet lemoncakes,
thinking about tall men of sciences, earth and sky.

An old love erases himself with fear, the bed unturned
his sheets pale, unused, and packed away.

I confused his light tweeds with some older garment,
caught his flying, chewing moths in my hope chest.

Until I remembered a second valise, another packed
case of strong breath-filled arm circles, a vast open bed.

His palms like lime-kilned rocks in sheets of wind,
freedom sparks between his fingers open ended.

These darker eyes see me now, explore palettes
entwine my dark and secret longings.

I know the physicals of science rather than its theory,
learn to smell and feel, in deep-quilted pasts reweaving.

drying off after snow

Pink naked afterbath thinking about the extreme physicality of snow,
The hard-soft, ice-warmed nature of things that fall from the sky.

Knowing the feel of my hands under skin and organs,
Mapping either side of the creative moments,
the everyday breaths, the openings and closings.

I hear silent longings paired with cacophonous speech,
Defying laws of discourse and gender
in shadowpaths of precious whiteskins.

in produce

You look me up in the vegetables,
trying not to stare at my bare hand.

We talk of exs and arts,
children, rutabaga, films.
Woman under tender skins.

Your hungry eyes scan the fruits,
melons, tomatoes, tomatillos
Russet hair like cornsilk.

And I become ripening produce,
two crisp apples and a d'anjou pear.
Reap ripe now.

I feel peeled open, bleeding,
in front of my gaping neighbors.

Run to checkout....
Safe.

seeing henry

I stand in a funeral parlor with a distant relative's name,
repeating memories from your mother's life
that transfer us out of our forty-five year old frames.

"I know you," you form your lips silently like fate,
our arms reach across a no-name crone in a walker
"You do," I say, thirty-three years late and full of symbols.

We say our names together, remembering younger bodies,
shorter selves with animal eyes imprinted on each other,
stacked like shelves of clean, never worn linen.

I see your sisters grown like mine into matrons and mavens,
and I know the reason I married the wrong Jewish man,
mistaking your dark eyes in his, similar voices calling me in.

It was you I wanted, sifting through exotic partners,
like Mah-jong pieces in ivory north winds,
I mistook the marionettes for the men, and that man for you.

You introduce your daughter, I tell you about mine,
I touch your welcome offers like promises never acted on,
You'll always be the first, never the last one,
You are not a piece but the uncut pattern.

As the requiem begins, the Kaddish undertones of your speech
draw your mother's face in yours, in memoriam in a synagogue,
I smile inside seeing your family between us again,
Like stands of cedars davining.

untitled

Don't name things - it captures the feelings from moments,
Desires form of mystery, winds plait - maybe, yes, yes.

Calling titles arrests the trickle of pomegranate juice,
Flavors roll off our tongues - bittersweet red tones.

My mouth licks fruits unknown, mashing my throat,
Things yet unnamed by men or hungry children.

My fingers long for flesh pulp meat fiber,
My eyes drink the orange colors of peachfuzz.

The young smell food from hunting mothers
Call us out of old longings and into veldts of space.

I turn the empty page to the silence of linguistics
No phrases, no prose, only paperweight landscapes of languages.

the still life of blackberries

1.

Greenthorned, wildgrown bushes
rising in May, spreading white petals over yellow throats
promising fruit, to birds and pickers who brave July brambles.

Purpled bloodclots, encircle black-hearted seeds
bursting with sweet imagination, flowing from maroon to indigo
offering clusters, sunwarmed under summer's branches.

Echos of screams, sour to sweet nature of the slow-riped
transformation of flower to fruit, seed to pulp
my dry tongue longs for rivulets of blackberry syrup.

2.

I am cajoled into a supermarket shopping frenzy
produce designs of California perfections, calling my hungry soul
I am seduced by the pinky beauty of skin under plastic coffins.

Resting in the top of my cart, a white-teethed boy pushing us
I walk tenderly, my vehicle ready for transportation to pulpy moments
But the cart overturns, the fruit mashes into rough blackened pavement.

Smearing the bloodless fruit, my eager fingers touch their tragedies
"I'll get more," he pants, running on catlegs to repick my losses
"It's the last one, you're lucky," I do not feel lucky. I am not satisfied.

With the new treasures on the seat, I plan ways to save the unbeautiful
secret in whipped cream and warm syrups, rich textured muffins and cakes
my willed fingers take their own life, searching for looted carcasses.

First I lick their bruise-colored skins, then bite the essences
like a child holding purple popsicles on the fourth of July
But my mouth makes an O, then widens in - "Sour" sounds.

The false berries, picked too early in foreign soils
can't be resurrected in sugarcream dreams, their inadequacy blooms
as true vine-ripe berries still work though nature's time cycle.

3.

Life rarely sends inside sweetness and outside beauty in the same body
a forced still life can't parallel something honestly formed
so sadly, I close my eyes to wait again for the breaths of July.

I'll take my tender fingers under the dark-prickly roadside vines
seeking the sharpened sweetness of blackberries eaten warm
shared only with a ripened lover, another home-grown beauty.

Having hidden his fruits, he waited for me in decades of seasons
safe, not picked too early or bruised juicy by ungentle hands
Now I mash purple globes into his mouth, sealing it with a rich Blackberry Kiss.

re covering

The epidermis lies, it lies
only at the top of beauty and pain.
It covers poorly, the bones, the blood
of life in cracks and hollows.
But it holds me in, them out
excavating only mapped surfaces.
Past cartographers charting, half-hearted
climbers over veiny roads and rivers.

Explorers return to themselves, looting
my extremities, showing vacation photos
fading prints of skin, receding
claw marks on my bending back.
Again and again, I fill, my pinkness
floods its scarred and damp territories.
I cover again, recover because inside
singing souls stay freshly untouched.

I'd stopped waiting, feigned engagements
and unions, fought possessive marauders.
Fully clothed against a steaming sun, I'm stunned
when you stand silently looking through me.
Poised for years, nails thickening, acids rising,
poems like well-wrapped sweets tease me.
Caught by external sirens, until midway through
the journey, under bites of cake, I see you.

Water eyes held in seatorn ones, you dip
into the core, below the second layers.
The subcutaneous parts of me, over and over
kneaded and scratched with no marks.
The unseen nature of me, begins the chorus
involuntary, natural, lyrical notes of self
Without plans, your polite bites, don't scar
but leave invisible tattoos, wanting more.

"So this is IT?" I whisper into your softness,
"After 40 years in this desert, this is the promise?"
"YES," you say in round consonants, "for me, too.
I know you from the inside, outside I know you..."
"I smell the spices of your woman's soul,
your fragile off-beating heart. YES, I know you, too."
You smile, take my hand, tell me you'll never
stay too long, never use me up.

I recover, pull my linen suit over your fingerprints,
straighten my glowing mind and hold my peace.
In the mirror I'm covered, covered
with golden rings on ears and wrists.
I smile at you in the mists,
these skins recall you to them.
I have my own nakedness under me, the
cloth and metal echoes of my Yesses.

seeing a former lover running

With what eyes
do I see you looking at me,
looking at you?

Blue stones and moon lights
connected to your linings,
sinews, arches.

With what fingers
did you touch me knowingly,
for each first time?

Long tapers burning me
as they studied my shapes.

With what feet
did you mold my skin
like hot wax on the sidewalk?

I still hear your silent,
silken depths
in virgin whispers.

on and on

Beware the tangled jaws of aching love
Its painful bites wrapping angles into yearning.

I miss a touch, I miss a deepening sigh
I want the knowledge that he's burning.

But a falseness sets like a broken ring
I must rise up to catch the glinting stone.

I'm bloody, weary, and pointed homeward
I smell the ether and hear deep voices ringing.

I'm half drunk with memories like still reflexes,
Each day moving further from that rasping grasp.

Alone at last, I see the black holes of him,
Hear only echoes of my bonding passed.

i begin again

I begin again
New phases of the moon in my life.
Tides catch silver water, churning foam
In the nets of my deepseaed self.

Over ebbed, wanting
The flow awake, but strangely quiet.
I want the divinity of the depths
My awful creatures long to swim.

I watch across smooth waters
Watercolors of azure or swan blues.
Carmine pains, ochre sands, cobalt skies
Wash into my seething shell.

My breath rises and swells
like the movement of the mother sea.
I open to her breath and search wholly
for a lighthouse on the rocks beyond.

watching eagles and nymphs

winter flying

I dream of you -
    bare tree fingers reading silent white sky.
Sounds of water -
    moving slowly in the lake of soul,
    the flow of emotion.

A nest tower-high -
    made of shaggy twigs promising safety.
We fly together -
    moving past earthy matters,
    soaring over foreign obligations.

We move in rhythm -
    light brown feathers and sharp wits.
We punctuate with separation -
    holding up the clear-air ceiling
    with well-muscled wings, on chilly breaths.

We flow into mystic distances -
    no limits, no differences, no geographies.

first eagle at reelfoot

Wind in the bareness, trees waiting
for dark feathers lifting in swampy moves.
You search with ice eyes on the water
head circling, fluid, and independent.

Your white tail magnetizes a cypress
your yellow beak smiling at fish.
You are god/goddess of lake and marsh
predator, progenitor, proprietor.

Life moves over your airwisp views
and under your flight patterns.
You write poetry with a wingspans
draw landscape with your hollow bones.

thundersnow
The Equinox

Woke early to a spring-weathered surprise,
heavy wet blankets of white glue.

This March, they say, is a new season,
my backyard freezes under thundered snows.

Under natural weights and frigid breath,
impressed distance, delicate wildflowers on glass.

In my back windowscope, trees bud up still,
sculptures cotton sogged and powder sugared.

Invisible footsteps on the roof promise more heft,
sags and groan waiting for the next sky to fall.

I'm caught between accumulating this white gold
or the promise of dripping green ingots and rainy skies.

If tomorrow really is the equinox as promised,
then is today just another winter memory?

I'll wait, reading myself for mixed weathers,
open to a thawed season coming soon.

I'll sit to drink fragrant coffees mixed with milk,
and warm bubbled oatmeal with brownsugar drifts.

I'll hear the thunder hit its magic godlike mark,
and follow the fall of light on roaring snow.

the geology of radnor

Sounds blended of voices, dogbarks, cars -
moving beyond the lake.
Pointing rustles like leaves strongly twisting -
but its winter.
We bend to listen, turning our ears to sounds -
like FM radios.

Its like-
water ripples of ice
caught on the crusted surface
in a duck-greyed pond
sunlight breaking the skin
into leaf-glass patterns
in pools of warm water bubble
of tiny geisers cracking.

Sounds like-
wind-chimed angels singing
from beneath the watertop
like hearts breaking free
songs of life pushing through
silent hard-worn rocks
of embracing islands dancing
frozen twigs and leftover leaves

Sketched like-
choruses of baby icewings
watercolors of joy and cerulean blue
the layers of liquid forming.

sense memories

My grandfather's ghost passes across us -
Echoing silent days under maples with tobacco wafts.
Summers walking behind his well-used plow -
Feeling headwaters of corn-streams in the earth.

His bone-heeled feet on bare oak floors -
Carrying rich bowls of French ice-cream
Wearing starched-striped pajamas smelling of rocks
Stirring Saturday night candies - brittle, fudge, divinity.

I know now that human-crafted something-will-happen feeling -
As I wait for the black car pulling up through buttercups
Imagining his forked-stick pointing to soon watered ground
Walked by witches, pigs, cows, hayfilled fairies dancing.

Left only is love memories from my childhood tongue
To open his hugs laden with the breath of farm animals
The gifts of natural silence forged at the family's roots
And imprinted on us all like immortality.

saturday afternoon warmings

Ice melts in cracks of leaf-veins on the pond.
Birds cross paths in the open flow, wings near water.

Feet touch fragrant forest leavings, intimate and familiar.
Wind breathes the bareness, skirts the edges of ice and water.

Signs chime tiny fairy chatter over the changing surfaces.
Faces mirror movements in watercolor soundbreaks of emotion.

Icesongs call us out of our wintered selves into dove waves.
Secret answers to long-pondered paradoxes float to air.

All this moves between us as I follow an endless smile across your face. I hear your silence warming and remember the sounds of my own voice.

the rape of the cypress

Running hard on flat sunset grasses,
the breeze cooling taut ankles,
her warming breath puffing close.
She sees a dark man walking forward
in even sure gaits like stallions,
Smiling round smiles so she knows him.

Always knows him before and after,
but surprised in this alien place,
not real, but more than real.
Laughing back into empty air
they watch the low sun.
Framed in delicate touches of bare trees.

Talking aloud softly over and over,
like forest creatures with secret names,
he beacons, urges her to the ancient swamp.
Black oil water pools under bones of giant trees
rushes moving, wind lingering.
Songs of capture, songs of nature.

He moves her back into the father cypress,
encircles the long-ribbed trunk,
ensnared, she closes baby-eyes to musty wetness.
The chesty scents of trees and mud
as he is wood and flesh behind her,
and she is naked to fiber and bone.

Branches in womb over arrowed breasts,
moving in tangos of birds and plants,
part of the pond's growth with earth.
Creating bodies vast and tall,
circling warmly on her belly,
she squats in sticky auburn leaves.

Birthing the moist roots of babies,
through perfect release in wind-dried motions,
she leaves alone but knows he's hiding in hardwoods
with dark, watery eyes in brown-lake colors.
Her strong knees lift up and down like pistons,
as she feels swamp mists rise on mud-red calves.

Leda is finally released,
Helen jogs along the lake.
The goddesses form to dance and dissolve,
the gods reseed to wait, the dance released
As the Sun goes DOWN,
and the Moon comes UP.

last night at the lake

Last night
there was a sky of many blues
Darkening colors
into iridescent indigos, infused.

You are colors
your open coat shows navy skins
the night sky opens
in the clear drops of your eyes.

it started with poetry

It started with poetry
the only voice reciting in a room of peach and blue.

It continued constantly
always turned up for personal moments or big events.

It was made of watching
your eyes following my gardens in harvests and tornadoes.

It was a gentle protection
unseemed and subtle on the surface, but ripening underneath.

Until I heard it crack open
felt you float to the top of warm splintering waters, seeking me.

frets in memory

sounds move up chords to clavicles
fingers dig for strings and toes
godknows I'm an aging instrument
reeking with symphonies and placentas

the capon slides up frets
is eaten in a vegetable stew
I hear echoes of screams and tunes
melanges of meat and me

winter light again lays fingernails on walls
my hands seek phantom warmth in whispers
I remember singers, their songs, their kneads
leaving yellow bruises and rhymes on my heart

hurricane ridge

In walk up an Olympic mountain in gold shorts and a rodeo headband,
matching stride and breath with a man of the rocks and woods.
We often stop to look up wildflowers in a pocket book bought at REI,
snapping our heavy backpacks behind us, leaning over log bridges.
Steady up, with snapped visuals across the ridges through firs,
we sip iodine water, stop for chocolate and sweaty kisses.

A bear stands up between us, posing for a picture as I swallow a scream,
then we watch him like an inchworm down a mountain into rushing
stream.
Bears swim without fear as I face the next terror - a log over his easy river,
deer wind across our path, blackhaired braveghosts run our campfields.
I dream of battles, open fires of red coals and desires, entrails read as
sacrifices,
I wake to soft trees blowing, night warlords subsided - I make cocoa on a
tiny fire.

The ridges call up spirits from my past, the past of other warriors,
we travel over the stream to find a grave under animal bones, marked
stones.
We leave these suncharred meadow fields, peeling the mountains from our
eyes,
closing former sleep battlements, risen from dust and meager provisions.
We return to our lushgreen home where we'll see color images of stormy
summer tops,
And rich evergreen dreams of high placed graves and bears and ridges.

writing my life

Writing the fictions of my life,
daily on the back of envelopes -
Not embossed initials over pink papers,
but junkmail pieces and make-do shreds.

My characters and words live,
between the sheets of life -
Not like my pen traveling over landscapes
beyond pages seeking memories and metaphors.

My feelings create these people, these places
but my words make them live -
Only I know their true seminal paper trails
others see them only cooked and cleaned.

Word processed, creamy skins emerge, slowly
the kernels, blowndust across old beginnings -
I make my silent scratching in torn languages
and they breath their own lives.

Now we all stand separate quiet
open to criticism -
breathing our separateness as if we'd never met
dreaming the pages of the book yet written.

springing forth

waiting

Spring is coming off the tight buds under old snow,
I smell the new breaths in hyacinth and forsythia,
I long for essential purples, tree yellows.

Holding underground green waiting for sunbaths,
watering in clouds silently readying.
I will see each narrow petal move apart.

Because this time,
I'll be watching for spring - early
I'll hear greening shoots moving up.

saints and ladies at christ the king

Sitting in metal chairs either side of Our Lady Goddess of Emotions, surrounded by city sounds, basketball, gym whistles, car lights on the shining asphalt.

I lost myself in the in-between of everyday conversation and psychic embrace, and all sound disappeared, visuals melded into the touch of breeze and breath.

I became young again under oak trees with barefeet,
I became innocent again, to no-speech bellylaugh bearhugs,
I became more myself by being all my selves.

The key lay between us, I felt its skeletal nature, smelled its metal sweat on my palm, seeing past base fear and hurt misted beyond golden lamps and familiar ghosts.

Sweet apples and rotten bananas mulched between us. We eat,
time stops so there was only endless time, real, encased.
Creatures, we dance in current bodies like saints and ladies.

Wakened statues merge with stainglassed martyrs, heroes
touch the two humans worshiping each other, we haunt,
Meet for the first time under watchful eyes of deities and dreams.

i know his name

I know his name, it is one syllable
I know the map to him, the many paths
I know him against great outside places
Surrounded by Indian blanket summers.

I am sure of the churchtower's bells
I know they'll ring together east and west.
I want his joys to chime themselves inside
dancing tango rhythms under his soles.

naked now

Without clothes, jewelry, makeup
    I place my body beside yours.
In clear daylight, in candled midnight
    I move my softness into yours.
We study scars, pockets, hollows in
    topologies of skin and muscle.
It can't all be perfect after years and years
    yet we've molded ours as perfect bodies.

There is a dance-music quality to us
    in our pulse beats and tender fingers.
The silence of strains long-ago, mesmerize
    rhythm and lyric, mythology and motion.
It's druid-like, native tongued, open-palmed
    worship for each other.
I see your light skinned back in the night air
    turning, pushing through sinews.

You walk toward me with arms in circles,
    ready to bring me close inside you
    beyond any nakedness into being only a sound.

frenzy and release

Washed with emotion this morning,
crying in a silent, childless car
under sheered cliff forces of internal waves.
I hear my full-bodied, rich root flow
resisting its separate, sparking intellect.

My creative core, earth-deep molten-moving
swirls skin taut on her stretched torso
a tortured victim across the rack.
The ebb of baby kisses cross-vein my neck
tidaling intensities over limp-handed stocks.

I rest. Expectant. Fussing about, frenzied
before the next birth; the welcome labor
knowing another wave will crash the cages open.
All my openings stretch beyond their shores
releasing me into the sea of intimacy or pain.

Sanguine language stops; body beats quicken
and the warm fruit ripens in my heated breath
a Universal build to release a newborn cry.
These open-souled comings and goings in life,
peeling away the core of humans touching all.

It brings us to each other's altars, naked again in Eden
want-wandering in innocence before drool-hasty biting
the seeds of experience and the fruit of tomorrow.
Naivete grows in little tides where coves of rocks hold cerulean seas,
inking ridges darken against night skies etched for mating.

Love multiplies, feeds itself on its own shells
a sky fills with light promises of dreams emerging free
found under fossils of creatures long before.
We know the antique sky is never only one color blue
the rhythm of the world is in each other moving.

We hear nature call in moments before we
taste the pulp of unchewed apples.
It will return, all. Go again. Again.
In then and now, ebb and flow
blue transparent love.

lincoln county landfill

In alien red earth places
garbage boils up from deadened sites
polluted by human sinnings
surrounded by forest turnings
designed by planet reactions

I walk certainly next to you
a perfect partner matched to fit
in stride and brain patterns
open to possibilities, burnings
scored with Edens remembered

We test land and streams at risk
we name flowers and trees in games
fresh cut woods and mossy logs
with lichen between green fingers
discovering as we play and hope

As we pass toxic lesions
measure glow-rock adhesions
listen for nature's arias
inside our chain sawed, ceil-skyed selves
a new world symphony opens

Overtones of deep-leached soil
and fouled and boweled belching
hawks fly mating patterns
above a smiling sky of boiling clouds
rainsoaked bottom grasses shoot green tenders

Life comes up again, again
despite humans poisons and horrors
fear of thundering progress halts
we'll let flow true nature
meanings with newborn words

We walk with soft hands held frankly
run through amber fields blown new
where nature again has its hold
delicately balances but real power
over humans, mistakes, and messes

We chase the flushed birds flying
to a rebuilding spring pond
from where we all came earlier
return over and over
as life continues, we begin again

The rain...forms its light
the white light of resurrection
remembered in the cells of plants
the hearts of lovers
the flight patterns of hawks

hibernation

Once, a young woman of twenty-four, shook her blondish braid
    on her creamed-white spine
Aware, a dark friend watched from his porch above with silent,
    searching eyes set fine
She mulched life, vegetables and fruit in the backyard bending
    overcreating stories from leftovers
He touched air lightly, filtering light from terror and refrain,
    creating possibilities from past pain
They wove away from each other's direct sights -
    she to drama and high-pitched crowds, he to foxed burrows
    undertombs and shrouds.

They waited in separate lives, unaware -
    he saved his deep gazes, she sadly cut her hair.
Twenty years pass quickly, calling them to families and partings -
    often to reappear in whispering silks and deep wools, sipping
champagne at others' weddings, lingering spirits in memorium
    children's ritual of bar mitzvahs and birthdays.
They drove the same streets for separate children, always ending
    in molded houses with unfamiliar spouses.

Yet nature's seeds are never truly dormant
    and life always seeks itself again.

Their midages rising and pasts dissolved, they walked an ice-rimmed
    February lake
Beginning to remember the dark boy watching the light girl's
    shadow
Water tuned sounds surge forth from former mudpacked graves
    So, they feel
early spring warmings, sleeping turtles moving, bare hardwoods
    rooting under murmuring songs.

Hibernation erased, embraced mated to all the world coming
    forth new again in ages, before and then, two people
Sliced open into many-tongued languages singing again
    they weave over each other's histories, page back over years returned
Become young and older, friend and lover, voyeur and discoverer
The rebirth of love, the compost of mistakes, and life grown converged.

Under a single beam of light woven in golden thread of bluenight stars,
    a deep-voiced symphony, the twenty-year euphony of liquid
    borne in waiting,
    hibernating
    and finally
    Remembered.

remembering you

Remembering you,
I purr.
Deep resonance from songs
lasting.
Mossy beds, inky nights
forever.
Our low breaths under
cover.
Back and forth, my hands
paw.
Places in your body fold
into me.
Scents rise from pink marsh
hollows.
Calling our names, insistently
waiting.
I hear your soft drawl, replying
before.
Years of silence before you
came.
Days of kittenish pacing before you
return.
A thousand moments of breath before you
again.

new edens

I picture you, another Adam choosing rocks in birth-drenched creeks
Splashing earth and water against your naked ankles, sunpink cheeks.
I stand in ferns watching spores and moss catch in my tangled, windborne dressing
Holding China-asters in my palms, offering anemones, green dragons, bloodroot's blessing.

We hunt and gather tender plants on the bank, together touching fertile under growing
Packing our babies into burlap blankets, wetting their roots, moving them in new garden sowing.
At home in Eden where the compost heats and the seed-happy birds dare ripe fruits open
We place your rivered rocks and dig warm holes for our wild children's new earths to soften.

I water each tiny bundle with rainmilk from a green can you once filled with irises dancing
You dig designs of bluebells, laces, grasses, lady's slippers under the birch tree's glancing.
As my evening approaches, my moon rises to smile on the daily new grown transplants
The white fires at twilight, the greens glow in evensong's seductive trances.

The light of your eyes promises morning sun to pull fresh roots to their suckling mother
My fingers pour liferich streams between rocks and roots, for you, the garden's father.
We all form statues in the darkening shadows, fading to sleeping stars awakening
Your hand seeks mine, sending memories of dust and wind, flesh and ribs not taken.

hands

An etched visual of those hands, well sculpted and clever
reveals only surface beauty, working bones and skins together.
But below the blood and tendon, these Michelangelo creatures
open tight shells, worn muscles into strains of stressless fractures.

They pry pain, dig emotions, work like silent bees to sting grains up
all negatives, crevices lay open like fresh daily fields of crops.
They dance, they prance, they feel though touchflow, greenlush calm
they free the demons, open the prisons with hard fingers and soft palms.

There is no gift so fine to give as these fine hands are constantly giving
no kisses, passions, embraces nearly capture their spirit for the living.
Their touch moves like water falling over mossy stone strewn streams
and I, the underbody, open physics to metaphysics of landscaped dreams.

I see your hands, their starfish fingers splayed, their curves in fleshy moons
teasing the skins of my brain and body, resurrecting me with god's finger tones.
I love these hands, as I'm no longer made of ungrateful clay or unyielding steel
so my metaphors pour honey in response to my hidden skinturned peals.

missing you

Missing you is strangely pleasurable like waiting for Christmas toys,
I gather longing, lust for crisp bundles and someday holiday joys.

I tie my love into coral ribbons, loops of satin round my waiting heart,
I want you but hold myself taut for another unwrapping to start.

I've stuffed this box with pink tissue, covered it with handmade paper silks,
I pile up to be torn open, teased from the middle, a broken bottle of milk.

I'm Pandora's pleasure, Santa's secrets, Venus's Looking Glass - my prizes
mount in the crinkling sounds, your chameleon eyes fired red full of
ornaments and surprise.

touch me

touch me, baby, reach across the air and take my skin in your fingers,
molded, kneaded, slapped and petted, I tame, but the wildness lingers.

your foggy eyes shroud my parts, recarving imperfections into sculptures,
exploding into shards of pink, layers dissolved into curves of futures.

mixed together, I lose myself in your worships, widening in tender tingles,
all my being alert, the once-caged heart awake and no longer single.

my soul warms under you, my blueprint skin catches light, ignites,
under your grazing hands, my core turns into white-keyed lightening.

floating to the top, you wind me in your arms like cobras from a tight
recoil
pipesung dances, separate again but waiting for another chance to boil.

that's where i love you

In between aisles of groceries, kisses in the dairy case, hugs in produce,
that's where I love you.

In between laps on the track, hard-mouthed touch and rasping bodies,
that's where I love you.

In deep woods on Mayday, sunshine on wine-tipped fingers feeling poems,
that's where I love you.

In rooms of strangers, looking at other's gazes but focusing quietly on me,
that's where I love you.

In passing cars, touching only palms full of electric light in orange and
blue,
that's where I love you.

Distant childhoods draw us unconsciously, neglect calls adieus, still
that's where I love you.

I remember your lonely apartment over mine, never able to quite speak,
but now, that's where I love you.

Middle age stretches us, gravity leads us scratching over bones and sinews,
yet that's where I love you.

All the near and pastlife traces gather, the future forms in smoke rings, and
that's where I love you.

past passing

Like Rip, I wake twenty years since
surrounded by familiar people and things,
but feeling not quite myself
unconnected to this woman's aged fingers.

Fingers which pick at the warp of yesterday
weaving through bright colors, unraveled-hiding
Hiding from my pain and staying cheery cold
in the colorschemes rather than my real life's tones.

Lifetones open old wounds of loss-mimed grief
covered over like cysts under surface skins
Skins forgotten in the heat of passing
blossomed beyond their soft, white buds.

Buds aborted before their fragrant flowers
could more than leave, in seeds blown away
Away my mind shuts over infinite maybes
Maybe now, I've opened that last door.

Doors framed in warm glorious colors
Colors like vermillion, carmine, indigo strong in visions
Visions like me and you, and all the pasts between
Between us like a shared mystery of dreams
Dreams like Van Winkle's yearning
Yearning for his wasted pasts
Pasts without all the nagging in them
Them and their false movements into the future

All our futures tense now.

the unlogicals of lovers

I ask you why you love me
you never say but touch my hungry finger.
My rationed brain wants answers
you only feed me kisses and arm rings.

I ask you why you hug me
with long liquid braces combining us hard
You tell me nothing, doing it again, again
until my heart opens like an almond cracking.

I ask you why you weren't here always
those years that wasted, never reclaimed
You tell me nothing matters now, except now
our fingers match, our breaths smoke fragrant air.

depths of moments

Anniversaries pass. Membranes lost in seas of sanguine tasks.
Only time absorbs life's spiral moments. Past the personal truths.
No masks. No clans. The truth of us standing alone and vital.

Holding substance in biological cesspools, life
becomes its own impossibilities. Unfiltered torrents. History
repeats. Refrains alienation, altercation, waste-solid fears.
Fears gathered beneath us in city sewers. Sacred
springs formed from former lovers' bitter-poison tears.

I focus the microscope of my own existence.
I connect to you in the surety of sunrises.
Freshwater rises like magic. The minutia recedes
as intensity heats our possibilities, dreams renew.
A day's events build the miracles of new castles.

* * *

Gathered in celebrations, piling-up holidays like memorized organs -
we float a raft, no longer tied to only me. We create safety.
Winter happens again, then a gentle thawing. Like
your first touch on my frozen bones. Cycles
churn under the warmth of your palms and changing eyes.

Long privacies of hands and souls move us forward. Constancy
remains like the currents of the next breath. We honor
the only true communion, one human loving another. Awash in
the basis, without lists or personalities. Feeling only heartbeats.
I glow inside, you warm my core, melting me more and more.

The ecology of love practiced at dinners and naps
maps the skeletal nature of our daily movements underwater.
Energies flow like river heads from two aquatic bodies. Separate
but mingling at sunset with silent waves touching. Gentle.
Contours of landscape and skein. Whole continents of flesh reborn.

I know these depths. Fathomed in muscle and rock. Tides
ebbing from our aging selves. Drawing sinews through ragged armholes.
I feel your hand when it's not there. Your strength
leaves imprints on me. Like symbols & characters of
texts written in the mutating human library.

My mind holds yours like my hands do.
My mouth seeks yours like our breaths do.
Liquids pass between us like whole seas.
My spirit knows yours from whole lives before.
Our dance on the pin's head; the only dance I can remember.

Today, as spring again fights for its life, our lives
stream up hill, resting together often.
I picture you in kitchens and offices, herding children
and teasing cats. Our separateness shrouds me.
I bloom now with the bed secret of Ulysses and Penelope -
Two olive-branches, two ever-growing bedposts
fed with living arteries of secret light and water.

feeling for natural elements

last night and this morning at sea

This spring winds in moments
crashing, carrying passion and confusion
along the paths of ancient comets in morning light.

Yesterday's torrents still echo
today, battles stir and images weave under
imprints of life and lore, masts of well-sailed history.

I prepare for the next hit
rest, basking in the blood orange sun
ready for another journey, another sailor's key.

My calloused fingers tremble
unwinding, a ball of knots patiently parted
circumnavigating the right to come and go.

The mission clears, weathers part
clouding, we breath together for a moment
all ships searching for sunset waters.

The greater ocean connects itself to earth
singing, caught together in light and dark
holding us to sandcastles and woodbeams.

sonnets for seafarers

Sea Level (1)

Her body wastes itself on ragged leas
windtorn cliffs of physical rage and pain.
Liquids ebb and flow, dashed diminished in vain
like moontides flowing over bloodsoaked seas.
Tempests take Her out, horizons call Her
mother tows pull home to sunwarmed sand.
Storms rob her essences, steal timeless ends
Laying bloated, waiting to rise or freeze.
Salt washes green eyes, seaweed tangles her
She prays for release, peace, a calmer night.
Lifting her full-memoried heart free
She sees a tall-armed sailor gathering light,
His oceaned self floats from hand-crafted symmetries;
he whispers words of safety, ends the weathered fight.

The Island (2)

A mythical place, rarely set at sea
this tiny island shores only for two.
Surrounded by tempests, leeward winds blew
this Adam and Eve to rest there, ever free.
All time swirled into their eyes, fixed solely
for another, beloved other "me."
Xanadu in divine heaven's mystery
Two seaed creatures, awash for years, finally
warm in each other's arms, lost in deep kisses.
They're not Miranda and Ferdinand exactly
nor star-crossed lovers hiding their distress.
They're just ordinary humans living meekly
but connected to each other, tethered to the universe
by a golden thread wrapped with love's key.

The Flow (3)

Wrapped in thick-wooled Connemara sweaters
they drift through inlets, wander coves of dreams.
Passing unnoted, moving through bluegreen seas
they flow to elsewheres while open to each other.
His greywater eyes hinge tight together,
waters mingling, dancing, waving forever.
Still hearing Her distant mother's siren screams,
she clasps hands hard, soul alight as beacon's beams.
Past lives call them from their lover's tether
whispering, "Best friend children on the beach."
But true dreams outlast any ocean's songs,
they're battle weary from what weathers teach.
This time, the mixing of breathless longings
flow through each other's night rain drenches.
The sailor and his beach bound gypsy row strong,
ever flowing through tears, storms, trenches.

Reborn in the Woods (4)

When seadrops fall on earthen places
and seedgerms scatter like grains of cornflowers,
the embattled mother-of-pearl over bower
births children in rosaried graces.
In a spring thicket of green-dressed towers
all sleep recumbent, fermenting in blood showers.
They, the seafarers, rest in growing places
crystal globe-lets flow, old eyes fall in shadow.
They welcome green children, leaf stalks throbbing,
root and feather make thickets tomorrow
contained new existence, no old sea sounding.
Weaving high foliage, kisses, lust's skin's farrow
pores breathe seaward, scents of home woods trembling.

Lovers Afar (5)

All lovers, starry eyed and star crossed,
Open their heavy purses, well-filled packs
to show the world their treasured sacks.
Romeo loved Juliet, despite the loss,
Abelard chose Eloise's truths embossed.
Today, real romance is stressed and tossed
and sea washed couples cover bare backs.
Nature's replaced itself with science's tunes,
Love's overcast by bankbooks and hot sex.
Material goods overshadow the moon,
lovers laugh at love, their muscles flex.
And body-built skins map complexes,
skystars doomfilled couples as bartered boons.

the good knight in a modern world

He stands over data and demons, wielding his computer as his sword,
his bespecked eyes absorb and flash, his fingers click and dash.
Thick-dark hair, soft khaki pants, worn t-shirts replace chainmail armor,
a ford instead of a steed, a brain rather than just muscled grit.
But hearts, the medieval and the modern, are faithful still
as chivalry and honor aren't yet dead, just mutated into virtual characters.

This new knight opens the next world with his soft voice and eager rhythms
rather than with weapons and undying other allegiances.
Lifecodes require precise navigation rather than colors of kingships,
new open-hearted men understand the female, carry no talisman tokens
Challenges joust consciences rather than bloody opponents, write verses rather than offences.
No Lancelot, but rather an Arthur and his best battlers combined,
flashing eyes cybersynapes ever readied to learn and forgive.
Like olden courtiers, his principles guide him over blueprinted skies
as insects fly to flame
His cheek turns, head bowed, past pains abated in present needs and beauty.
Romantic, yes, and maybe old-worldly, as this new age still needs nobility
So this new knight, middle-aged wise, leads the charge to change
bleeding in imagination and soul—heeding the next century's call.

my tribe

Many years ago, adults circled free,
forming a spray of single hatfeathers,
eating and drinking on fortnights
together extending their family.

Celebrating new weddings, deaths, births
reformed between the vast repasts,
males and females, older and younger
friends in present and gathering pasts.

Shrimp and pork, vegetarian and alcoholic
kosher, microbiotic to exotic fare,
drinking wine, no wine, and fancy waters
cares and food broken and shared.

Now, more than two decades later
we form a richer circle around a rounder table,
witnesses to each other's lives and lovers
grown fat from storing dinner groups' fables.

Still, meeting and eating on Thursday nights
prime time played in a newfound clan turning
the best of human quilts sewn minute to minute
woven in the fruit of many-dinnered learning.

losing aaron

Aaron-

A prince of intricacy, brain and wit like quicksilver, he turned phrases
or game pieces with speed and grace, impishly winking and glowing with
fun.
A prophet of humanism, deep-rooted in religious contexts, his written
words
moved away from Brother Moses' tablets into daily newspaper tableaus.
A joy-for-lifer, the infectious tickles of his humor still pass back and forth,
all cast from the green nets of his intellect, the bricked bonds of his
intimacies.
A professor of living, a lover of history and jokes, he reached across the
internet,
through culture and space, touching thousands of fellow explorers.
A poet of politics, a learned rabbi called him brilliant, a tough
newswoman cried
to learn we'd no longer hear or read his latest spiritual jeremiad.

This man who'd flown fifty war missions, and lost his left-ear's hearing
could still hear the sound of a child thinking or a society reaching for
meanings.
This man who could hum most operas or recite lyrics from Jefferson or
Genesis,
could still sing the praises of his last day's reading or his wife and friends.
This man's personal renaissance had made him actor, seller, thinker, and
writer,
going beyond his village, beyond his tribes, beyond his own beginnings.
This man, propelled by Language, worshipped at the altar of inquiry
his mind and heart open to life's absurd and unexpected data and delights.
This man's viewpoints—from skeptic word-smith to aging wunderkind—
made us laugh and wonder at the interwoven webs of humanity we share.

Aaron's looks - a jester smiling, the scholar of scrabble, the knight of
opinion
Aaron's voice - an echo even now, sounding like Schubert's suites in all
of us.
This Spring remembers, renews its yellow tulips and soft-balled greens.
No knots end - the influence of this one man's texts and hugs never end,
their warp and strength connecting us as the humans left.
No gathering ends - the celebrations he taught us with contexts and
conversations.
No relations end - his crayon-colored familial and filial fabrics woven
with his fingers, cupped hands giving us all the sips of his life and love.
Aaron's still here in turns of notes and arguments, grinning at us for six
o'clock suppers or bites of sweets.
Aaron's still here, as long as we are still here, as long as his words and
ways resound, bound between the covers and pages of our minds.

searching cemeteries

A goateed man with an earring, "Can I help?"
I open my hands, my mouth says, "No, I'm looking for relatives' names."
Names like Champagne, Winston, Ducotie—
"I know the place," the swain speaks, moves between the crypts.

In the new rows of this century, we tour the dead,
Lafayette Cemetery #1, Est. 1833 — full of silent, concrete houses.
None there from my list, then, engraved is MARSHALL, "Were you mine?"
Christine and George, B1869, D1921 —could you haunt me as Norman
kin?

New Orleans is languid, full of terror and sun -
Waiting for the South to Rise Again, I sip Hurricanes and eat tainted
oysters.
The swarthy man behind me, angrogynous and necrophalic
I won't find myself in these bones but rather in the flesh of my
imagination.

my life is like jazz

Syncopated
sucking richness from an off-beat heart.
A sudden word
dances me into the roaring night.
I taste the sauce
of a Creole master's gumbo spoon.
Sounds of brass horns
Tuba, sax, trumpets in my belly.
It blends and drums
messages from the streets of voodoo souls.

the ghosts of vicksburg

Mad river winds and constant sun
make me chilly warm.
Old ghosts of generals and ladies dance -
appear in decadent buildings between the bricks.
History and horror hold hands -
he straightens his sword; she holds bloody crinoline.

Surface life is bitter with old anchors still tied
to prewar houses growing antique roses
between seedy warehouses and river barns.
This is no-where and used-to-be,
but still holds pulses under river breezes
filled with musks of moss and bones.

Some gray-toned soldiers sat on this hill
some laden barges tugged through that muck
in these deified pasts swarming under winter light.
I crack my spectacles to see them -
the ball-gowned Scarlets turned pageant queens
waiting for horses hooves and captain's eyes.

Is there something yet to claim
in the battlement of then and the cemetery of now?
The old mansions stand, asking for coins
in between the modern shacks and ordinary ranches.
Visible etches of ghosts from magnolia parlors
reflected in vacant downtown windows and beauty parlors.

Vicksburg revisited; time retreats
and the parallel lives compete for space
in the clean white lines of the graveyard
and the muddy silt of the rivers converged.
The town wills its visibility
like a slave on the block forever remembering.

natchez

Rainwater flows down time-frozen paths
magnolias bend with heavy drops.
Scents of hooped and hard-laced ladies
drape over fainting couches, breathing wet and heavy.
Swaying, desperate over spiral stairs -
waiting for a uniformed man to render their full-teastered dreams.

Now reduced to pour silverpots of hope and tears
forever repeated in parades of tourists.
Sifting through antebellum stuff, worshiping the antiques,
human yearnings and human-made things.
Houses stand buttressed by old-money.
Clubs or homes show diminished circumstance, peeling wallpaper.

Trellises of roses lead to long lawns, gazebos on the Mississipi
forgotten flowers stand alone under decaying walls-
Holding history like cisterns, the river evercalling like a lover,
uncovered pieces on a wartorn grave of uncut stone
Adrift from glacier beginnings, uncultivated and alone,
geology and history conspire against the humans.

Cotillion dresses in closetbags stand ready for current battles
new hewn belles soften their voices to fight wars
for space and real estate, making millions
or holding the line of bed-and-breakfasts and good help.
Slaves to the Old South, culture growing like mold on live oaks,
barracks of Yankees still marching forward past Sherman's lines
over Grant's four-posters, repeated rapes in white and black.

Natchez lies bleeding; as history repeats itself
in the juxtapositions of then and now
opening old wounds of powder and blood.
Architecture holds new redoubtments, calling for coins of preservation,
Over Tara or Longwood, life undoes its stays before it expires,
the pilgrimage of Northern aggression continues, loops a matinee.
Time is captured in a glass overturned with a honeyglass catching flies.

riding on red clay

A wedding guest, unrelated to bride or groom sided clans -
I wandered here over waves of sandy soil washed by pinebreezes.
I see an isolated man, bigger than the rest, with crusty hands -
his eyes like seapools holding silent currents of Georgia skies.
We share the surreal moments of outsiders caught under glass, targetfans -
surrounded by sequin dresses unfurling in blacktailed slow dances.

He speaks of the tight pinecones on red clay, strawgrounds -
outside his ramshackle home, homesteaded under the low river woods
sap lined with sweetgum and deep blue junipers cracked with sounds -
So my soles feel needles, my eyes fill with earth-like human contours
lined by gentle bones of gentle men's souls set with humble crowns -
bodies baked in redbrick ovens, framed by cedar forests, damp and old.

As the bride dances, I hear long songs from this other guest -
his voice a staccato, rapid fire of Southern rifles repeated, repossessed
by distant soldiers, hunters, and gentlemen of skeet with whiskey breaths -
Then the white veil removed, she undulates like a heron flying at sunset,
body conscious under nets of lace and tulle, her future's blessed -
with new tight skins later reddened under the August burns and wrinkled
mirrors.

The scrub brush beauty I'd missed in my first views of this land -
seduces me now with its sameness, like imprints of all human forms
waves grasses over clay, eyes like cauldrons virgins find -
The sense of order and control in vast geographies. Calls us to
where women offer scepters of skin, and the men hold earthmade sand.
I repeat refrains, put my hand to His, to ride the red clay dance floor
behind the bride again and again.

a room full of clocks

Tic and pull, pushing seconds forward
back like waves of time.
Clocking the next phase, a metronome
of cacaphany in up and down.

Little deaths, each minute of life gone
machines watch me
Pretending to be good soldiers, stiff hands
pointing to the end of something.

i am from every place

I am from every place, no scenery is unknown
the same sky hangs its curtains over me
only colors change from white gauze to black silks

It is the same earth, my feet feel its shapes
the shifts of animals and plants and humans
scratching for food, love, webs of existence

The same hours come again, the years repeat
ennui calls my name, the wind catches my red scarf
and the sky's streaked with yellow thorns

The scenery darkens, builds to emotion
seawaves stir, birds shelter on limerocks, and I'm here
smelling distances and remembered salty love

bastet 600 b.c.

Feline silhouettes, like a tall black woman with golden earrings
Sitting Buddha-like, a wise one hearing echoes.
Do you hear the songs of your sisters?
Winding up Venetian canals or Irish alleys, a soul
Looking for a body, the terrors of forage on your face.
Tell me, are you a goddess men prefer?
Lasting beyond the civilizations you visited, abandoned in
Egypt, China, and Rome, Forgotten like other females.
I remind you of Maya, Alice, and Emma.
And you, smile that semicircle smile
Your secrets, passed to all women of wisdom.